P H I L I P P I N E
W I L D L I F E

Produced by JOSE MA. LORENZO P. TAN

Bookmark

COPYRIGHT © 1992, by Bookmark, Inc. ◆ 264 Vito Cruz Ext., Makati, Metro Manila ◆ Tels. 86-80-61 to 64 ◆ Book design by Beth Parrocha with the help of F. Doctolero ◆ Printed by Vera-Reyes ◆ Color separation by Scanatronic ◆
◆ ISBN 971-569-058-0

CONTENTS

The Philippine archipelago is home to an unbelievable number of unique and rare animals. In the matter of wildlife, this is a land of absolutes. These islands have the largest and smallest fishes in the world—the Whale Shark on one hand and *Pandaka Pygmaea*, a miniature goby on the other. A 21-foot Estuarine Crocodile from the Philippines holds the distinction of being the longest crocodile ever captured. (The Agassiz Museum at Harvard reportedly houses its skull.) With a wingspan of nearly two meters, the Philippine Eagle is one of the largest, and most majestic birds of prey in the world. The Giant Clam, *Tridacna gigas*, is the largest bivalve ever evolved. The largest living Tridacna on record is under the care of the Calauit Wildlife Sanctuary in Palawan. At 32 feet, the Reticulated Python is the longest snake in the world. It is also found in the Philippines.

These islands are home to a host of unique mammals, such as the Philippine Tarsier, the Palawan Bearcat, the Flying Lemur, the Mouse Deer, the Dugong, the Tamaraw of Mindoro and the Cloud Rat from the Gran Cordillera Central. The list of unusual animals goes on and on: the Peacock Pheasant—unique to Palawan, the Chambered Nautilus, the Sailfin Lizard, the King Cobra—largest poisonous snake in the world, The Coconut Crab—*Tatus*, the Luzon Bleeding Heart Dove and *Hydrophis semperi* of Taal Lake—the only known freshwater sea snake in the world. It is a tremendous collection, the stuff of legends. And yet, so few know so little about Philippine wildlife. Many of us grow up knowing how to recognize lions, elephants and tigers. Very few of us, however, know what a lemur, or a tarsier, or a dugong looks like. Can we hope to save animals that we cannot even identify?

This book was published to give more people the opportunity to get to know and appreciate Philippine wildlife. The animals in this book are arranged by habitat. This format has been selected to emphasize that destruction of natural habitats—such as forests, wetlands, and reefs—will inevitably lead to the extinction of all the wildlife that live there.

The animals in this book all occur naturally in the Philippines. A number can also be found in other countries of Asia, Africa and Europe. Some of them, however, such as the Philippine Eagle, the Tamaraw, the Peacock Pheasant, and the Cloud Rat, are endemic and have been recorded nowhere else in the world. Unfortunately, many of these unique animals are endangered. It is becoming increasingly more difficult to locate them in the wild. Victims of ignorance, apathy, politics and greed, they are disappearing as their habitats are destroyed by man.

A recent study by the Haribon Foundation lists 1966 species of land-based animals found in the Philippines. This book features less than 100. It does not strive to be definitive or complete. It merely provides a glimpse of some of the more well-known and the most endangered. These animals must be saved. Man will be the ultimate beneficiary of any effort to save these animals and their habitats. Whether he admits it or not he, too, depends on the forests, the wetlands and the reefs to live. Unless something meaningful is done soon, these habitats will cease to exist. We will lose these priceless living treasures that make the Philippines a special place. And, extinction is forever.

The PUBLISHERS

A lush
tropical belt extends
from Central and South America,
across Central Africa, to Southeast Asia and the
islands of the Pacific. This is the realm of the rainforest.
Millions of species of flora and fauna—over half of the world's plants
and animals—are part of this vast ecosystem. The rainforest has been referred to
as the "lungs of the Earth". And yet, for some inexplicable reason, man is destroying the
rainforest at a rate estimated to run as high as 77,000 square miles each year. At this rate, we will
completely destroy the Earth's rainforests along with the innumerable species that inhabit them by the middle of
the next century. This is not far-fetched. In the 1930's, the Philippines had 16 million hectares of old-growth
forest. In less than 60 years, close to 95% of these forests have been wiped out. We have less than a million hectares of
old-growth forest left today. Scientists estimate that a great number of plant and animal species in the rainforest remain
undiscovered. An untold number of plants and animals are, therefore, being eliminated even before scientists
have had a chance to catalog and study them. The loss is incalculable. Tropical forests are rich with life both
in number and variety. This biodiversity is unique in the world. A typical four-square-mile area of
rainforest contains as many as 1,500 species of flowering plants, 750 of trees, 125 of mammals,
400 of birds, 100 of reptiles, 60 of amphibians and 150 of butterflies. Many of
these are endemic, or exclusive, to their native corner of the jungle.
Destruction of their section of rainforest renders them
instantly vulnerable to extinction. This is happening
today, in the rainforests of the Philippines and all over the
world.

ANIMALS *of the* FOREST

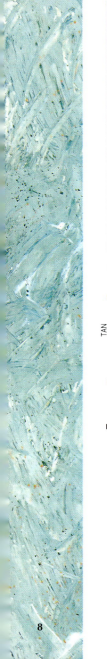

TAN

CRIMSON-BACKED WOODPECKER

Pithecophaga jefferyi

PHILIPPINE ◆ EAGLE

Haribon, Manaol

Endemic. 100 - 300 animals left

Class: Aves

Size: 97.6 to 102.6 cm,

2 m wingspan

Range: Reported in Leyte, Samar,

Sierra Madre Range & Mindanao only

ENDANGERED

. . . .

This is the great eagle of Asia—one of the largest birds of prey in the world. It is found only in the Philippines. There are barely 100 of these giant eagles left in the wild because of hunting and loss of forest habitat. Attempts have been made to breed this bird in captivity. In 1992, these efforts bore fruit. Much work, however, remains to be done.

HARIBON FILE

Tarsius syrichta

PHILIPPINE ◆ TARSIER

Mago, Mamag

Endemic

Class: Mammalia

Size: 61.5 to 67.9 cm

Range: Reported in Leyte, Samar,

Bohol & Mindanao only

When considered in proportion to its body, the Tarsier's eyes are the biggest among all animals. They are, however, fixed in their sockets and cannot move. To see sideways, a tarsier must turn its head. Fortunately, tarsiers can turn their heads 180 degrees. They also have paper thin ears that can be twisted to focus on a particular sound. They are phenomenal leapers and nocturnal hunters. These animals have been reported in the forests of Bohol, Leyte, Samar and Mindanao. Other species are also found in Borneo and Sumatra. Efforts to breed them in captivity have so far been unsuccessful.

-TAN

MONITOR ◆ LIZARD

TAN

RETICULATED PYTHON

This is the longest snake in the world. It is not unique to the Philippines, however, and can be found in various islands of the Indo-Malayan region. A specimen captured in Palawan was found to have a 60-kilo wild boar in its stomach.

TAN

CRMF FILE

TAN

PHILIPPINE ◆ COCKATOO

TAN

BLUE ◆ NAPED
P A R R O T

RUFOUS ◆ HORNBILL

Bubalus mindorensis

TAMARAW

Endemic

Class: Mammalia

Height: 100 to 120 cm at shoulder

Range: Mindoro only

This animal is found only on the island of Mindoro. Widely known for its ferocity, it has been hunted for many years and is now severely endangered. A gene pool was established in an effort to halt the rapid depletion of tamaraws. So far, it has not been successful.

SERPENT ◆ EAGLE

CUCKOO • DOVE

BLACK-BILLED COLETO

GREEN • IMPERIAL • PIGEON

WILD ◆ PIG

SCALY ◆ ANTEATER
(P A N G O L I N)

This toothless, nocturnal mammal feeds
exclusively on ants and termites. It has
large claws which it uses to dig into termite
mounds. When disturbed, it defends itself
by rolling up into a scaly ball. One species
is found in Palawan. Six other species
are found in some parts of Asia and Africa.

ENDEMIC

TAN

Polyplectron emphanum

PALAWAN
PEACOCK ◆ PHEASANT

Tandikan

RARE, Endemic

Size: 32 to 36 cm

Range: Palawan only

ENDANGERED

This beautiful bird is found only on the island of Palawan. It is extremely rare. Although several specimens can be found in local zoos, no successful captive breeding program exists.

Gallicolumba luzonica

LUZON BLEEDING-HEART DOVE

Puñ alada

INDETERMINATE, Endemic

Class: Aves

Size: 20 to 25 cm

Range: Luzon, Polillo, Negros, Mindanao, Basilan, Samar, Leyte, Mindoro

. . . .

Several species and sub-species of this endangered bird exist. It has been reported in Luzon, Polillo, Negros, Mindanao, Basilan, Samar and Leyte.

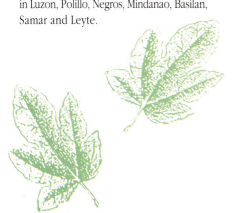

TAN

TAN

MOUSE • DEER

Like the bearcat, several species of Mouse Deer are found in other countries of the Indo-Malayan Region. This specimen was photographed at the captive breeding enclosure at the Calauit Wildlife Sanctuary.

TAN

NICOBAR ◆ PIGEON

Pteropus luecopterus

PHILIPPINE WHITE ◆ WINGED FLYING ◆ FOX

Paniki

ENDANGERED

Class: Mammalia

Size: 36 cm

Range: Reported in Catanduanes,
Tawi-tawi, Mindanao, Samar & Leyte

Manila Zoo, Manila

. . . .

Flying foxes, or fruit bats, do not live in caves. Rather, they live in tree tops in communal roosts numbering in the thousands. In the evenings, they set off in groups travelling as far as 70 kilometers in search of food. This is one of many species of flying foxes found in the Philippines. It has become increasingly rare. This specimen is from the captive breeding project of Silliman University on the slopes of Mt. Talinis in the island of Negros.

TAN

TAN

PALAWAN • BEARCAT

This animal comes from Palawan. It is also found, in other countries of the Indo-Malayan Region. This particular specimen is "BC"—the most amiable among the bearcats of the Calauit Sanctuary.

TAN

COCONUT ◆ CRAB

This specimen was photographed in the Batanes Islands. Coconut crabs, also called Robber Crabs, are hatched by the water edge as larvae. As they reach maturity, they leave the sea and live on land. They are not unique to the Philippines and can still be found in many of the more isolated islands of the Indo-Pacific.

Cynocephalus volans

FLYING ◆ LEMUR

Kaguang

Endemic

Class: Mammalia

Length: 66 cms

Range: Mindanao, Samar,

Leyte & Bohol, Indo-Malayan Region.

. . . .

Although the flying lemur, or colugo, is also found in other parts of Southeast Asia, the Philippine species is acknowledged to be distinct from those that occur elsewhere in the region. It hangs from trees during the day using its furred cloak of skin as camouflage. At night, it glides from tree to tree to forage for food. The female of the species is distinguished from the male by a bright yellow stripe that runs down the middle of her face. These specimens come from a captive breeding program of ERDB at Mt. Makiling in Los Baños.

TAN

CLOUD ◆ RAT

This animal has been reported in Rizal and Laguna. Several other varieties of Cloud Rats have been recorded. A spectacular species, *Crateromys schadenbergi*, comes from the mountains of Benguet and Banaue and has a long bushy tail which other cloud rats do not have. These specimens were from ERDB on Mt. Makiling.

TAN

PALAWAN ◆ PORCUPINE

Grasses dominate vast areas between the Earth's forest and desert zones. These expanses range from the tropical savannas of Africa and South America to the temperate prairies and steppes of North America and Eurasia. There are some 10,000 known species of grasses in the world, making it one of the largest plant families on Earth. Grasses can survive low rainfall, grazing, mowing, fire and hot sun. All they need to thrive is abundant light.   They are very suitable vegetation for arid lands because their extensive root systems can absorb water and mineral salts from a wide area. These same root systems bind the soil particles together, preventing their loss to wind or water erosion and creating a stable environment in which other plants and animals can live. A rich assemblage of animals has adapted to survive in these regions, creating an extensive grassland food chain. This food chain starts with the sun, since all plants need the sun for photosynthesis. The herbivores live by exploiting the plants of the grasslands. They also help maintain the vigor of the grasses by grazing and fertilizing and by eating or trampling down the woody shoots which threaten to invade the plains. The predators, in turn, thin out the herbivores, thus preventing overgrazing of the grasslands. After predators, it is the turn of the scavengers. They clean up what the predators leave behind. The food chain does not end here, in fact it is a cycle. All waste products decompose and return to the soil. The decomposers, those minute creatures that are responsible for this process, are invisible to the naked eye.   These bacteria, protozoa and fungi create the rich medium which then give life and vigor to a new growth of grasses.   Several centuries ago, over forty percent of the Earth's land surface was covered with natural grasslands. Today, only about half of these remain, most of them in Africa. In most grasslands of the world, man has decimated the wildlife and converted the land to his own use with no regard for the ecological consequences of his actions. Most of the animals that have been closely linked with natural grasslands for millions of years have been reduced to a few sparse herds in remote corners of the world. As human populations in these areas grow, so the wild herds dwindle further. Like other major habitats, the grasslands play a key role in maintaining the balance of life on Earth.   This planet's capacity to support life is rapidly dimi- nishing. And man, once again, is to blame.

ANIMALS *of the* GRASSLANDS

CALAMIAN ◆ DEER

These deer come from a group of islands in northern Palawan called the Calamianes. They are classified as threatened. This large buck is one among 600 deer under the protection of the Calauit Wildlife Sanctuary.

ENDEMIC

Cervus alfredi

VISAYAN ◆ SPOTTED DEER

Usa

Endemic

Class: Mammalia

Height: 139 to 142 cm at the shoulder

Range: Reported on Negros,

Leyte & Samar only

. . . .

Most young deer are born with spots which they lose as they mature. This deer retains its spots even when full grown. It is found only on certain islands of the Visayas and is severely endangered. These specimens are from the captive breeding program of Silliman University.

TAN

TAN

PHILIPPINE
HORNED ◆ OWL

CRESTED ◆ MYNAH

TAN

GRASS ◆ OWL

TAN

CATTLE ◆ EGRET

TAN

BLACK ◆ NAPED ◆ ORIOLE

34

PALM ◆ CIVET

TAN

TAN

LEOPARD ◆ CAT

This is the smallest and most common species of wildcat found in the Indo-Pacific region. It is often seen around farms and villages.

Coral reefs are found in two
main areas of the world's oceans: the west Atlantic, from
Bermuda to the coast of Brazil and the Indo-Pacific region from the coast of East Africa
to Southeast Asia and beyond to Hawaii and the eastern Pacific. Coral reefs have been called the "rain
forests of the sea". They are usually found only in tropical seas. There are three basic types of reefs: fringe reefs,
which extend outward from the shore into the water; barrier reefs, which are farther from land and separated from the
shore by a lagoon; and atolls, independent ring-shaped reefs that arise in very deep water from land and enclose a lagoon. Nearly
all atolls are in the Indo-Pacific. Reefs are formed through the symbiotic relationship that exists between coral polyps and a single-celled
algae called *zooxanthellae*, which live within the tissue of the polyps, absorbing both sunlight and nutrients. Polyps manufacture calcium
carbonate to make up their external skeletons. Photo-synthesis in the algae enhances calcification of the
skeletons. Without sunlight, photosynthesis cannot occur. Without zooxanthellae, polyps would not be able to
continue building reefs. A complex system of marine life depends on the organic matter produced by the inter-
action of a coral reef's many inhabitants. They feed, seek shelter, breed and spawn here as well. A single coral reef can
support as many as 3,000 different species. Like rainforests, however, coral reefs face widespread destruction. There is no one cause that
can be isolated as the primary threat to coral reefs. The reefs of the world face a multitude of dangers. A simple change in water
temperature due to increased pollution or global warming can drive zooxanthellae away and cause bleaching. Commercial fishing,
especially muro-ami and other destructive fishing techniques, can upset the delicate balance of life on a reef by reducing the
number of algae-consuming fish. Sediment in the water, due to deforestation, coastal development or sewage also
destroy reefs. These, and any other threat to the reef, such as dynamite fishing, the use of cyanide and other
poisons, oil spills and the gathering and sale of coral automatically become a threat to the vast ecosystem they nurture. 80% of all known coral species in the world are found in the
Philippines. However, barely 5% of Philippine coral reefs
remain in excellent condition.

ANIMALS *of the* CORAL REEFS *and* SEAS

BINAMIRA

GIANT ◆ CLAM

This is the largest bivalve in the world. Although it has no arms, legs, tentacles, tongue or tail, it makes its own food and feeds itself. The largest living Tridacna on record is under the care of the Calauit Wildlife Sanctuary in Palawan.

ENDANGERED

Dugong dugon

DUGONG

Duyong

Class: Mammalia

Range: Reported in Palawan,

Bicol and Samar

. . . .

This marine mammal is thought to be the source of mermaid stories. It has been reported in Palawan, Bicol, Samar and off the northeastern coast of Luzon. Dugongs are also called sea cows because of the way they graze on sea grass in the shallows. Once plentiful, they have been decimated in Philippine waters. There is no program to protect the Dugong.

BINAMIRA

Eretmochelys imbricata

HAWKSBILL ◆ TURTLE

Pawikan, Karaan

Class: Reptilia

Length: 70 to 75 cm

Range: Tropic Seas

Like the Green Sea Turtle, this animal is found in all tropic seas. Unfortunately, it too has become quite rare in Philippine waters. To distinguish this turtle from the Green Sea, one need only compare their shells. Turtles have been reported in Mindoro, Zamboanga, Baguan Tagunab, Barcauan Island, Cagayan de Tawi-tawi, Palawan and off Antique. A number of sea turtle protection programs exist.

WHALE ◆ SHARK

This is the largest fish in the world—sometimes measuring fifty feet in length. (Whales are mammals, not fish.) This is also the largest shark in the world, but believe it or not, it has no teeth. Like whales, these animals strain the sea for tiny marine organisms. They are found in the Philippines and in all tropic seas.

BINAMIRA

43

BINAMIRA

Chelonia mydas

GREEN ◆ SEA ◆ TURTLE

Pawikan

Class: Reptilia

Length: 75 to 80 cm

Range: Tropic Seas

. . . .

This turtle is found in all tropic seas. It has become increasingly difficult, however, to find them in Philippine waters due to poaching. This specimen was photographed at a holding pen off Calauit.

CUTTLEFISH

44

MANTA ◆ RAY

The Manta or devilfish has been known to grow to as much as 20 feet across. It is found in all tropical seas and around many islands of the Philippines. Mantas are filter feeders that live on floating shoals of tiny crustaceans and fish. Pamilacan, an island off Bohol, is known even today as the nesting place of Manta rays.

BLUE ◆ SPOTTED
STING ◆ RAY

BINAMIRA

BINAMIRA

CLEANER ◆ SHRIMP

This tiny animal can be called the toothbrush of the sea. He clambers into the mouths of larger marine animals like groupers or eels and picks out bits of food stuck in their teeth. In return for the service, the big fish keep their mouths open when the shrimp is inside.

BINAMIRA

MORAY ◆ EEL

OCTOPUS

BINAMIRA

FROGFISH

CLOWN ◆ ANEMONEFISH

SAVE · THE · CORALS

PORCUPINE ◆ GLOBEFISH

BINAMIRA

BINAMIRA

UNICORN ◆ SURGEONFISH

GIANT ◆ GROUPER

Philippine fisherfolk had long spoken of groupers as large as cars that swallowed skin divers whole. They are more fearful of these animals than they are of sharks. This specimen beached itself in Palawan. A photo is one good way of proving that these submarine giants do exist.

RED◆GROUPER

BINAMIRA

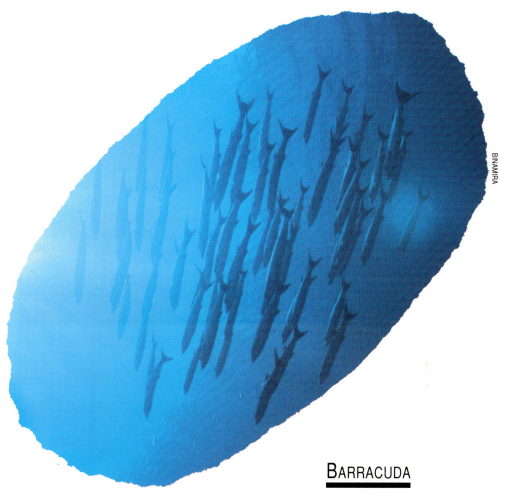

BINAMIRA

CRMF FILE

BARRACUDA

LIONFISH

BINAMIRA

B A N D E D
SEA ◆ SNAKE

These snakes are known to be more poisonous than cobras. A variety of sea snake, *Hydrophis semperi*, has entered and adapted to the waters of Taal Lake in Luzon. It is the only species of sea snake in the world that inhabits fresh water.

SMOOTH TRUNKFISH

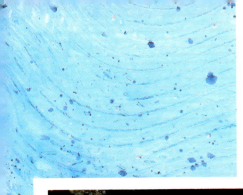

CHRISTMAS TREE ◆ WORM

CROWN ◆ OF ◆ THORNS
STARFISH

JONES

SEA ◆ URCHIN

FEATHER ◆ STAR

LONG-SPINED
BLACK ◆ SEA ◆ URCHIN

BINAMIRA.

TIGER ◆ COWRIE

BINAMIRA

RINAMIRA

CHAMBERED NAUTILUS

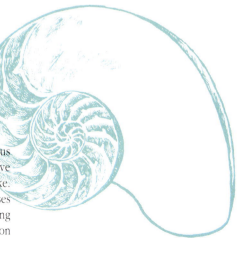

Many have seen the shell of this curious marine creature. Few, however, have ever seen how the animal itself looks like. This is a very rare photograph. Nautiluses normally linger in very deep water, rising or descending through the use of flotation chambers found in their shells.

I. TAN

BINAMIRA

BINAMIRA

BINAMIRA

S·A·V·E · THE · MANGROVES

There are more than 100 types of wetland. The term can refer to swamps, marshes, ponds, mud flats and many other areas with water-logged soil or a shallow layer of water. Wetlands provide a host of ecological benefits. Coastal wetlands, for example, act as buffers during storms.   They protect the coastline from wind and waves and act as a "storm shelter" for fish and other forms of marine life. Inland marshes act like a sponge, absorbing and slowing flood waters. They also support freshwater species of fish. Wetland plants act like filters, absorbing noxious contaminants. Silt from floods settle at the base of wetland plants, and protect aquatic animals and rivers from pollutants. Coastal mangrove swamps produce most of the seafood we eat—almost 66% of fish caught worldwide are hatched in tidal zones.   Wetlands provide food and shelter for a variety of mammals and habitats for millions of waterfowl and other birds. Traditionally, wetlands were considered nuisances to be filled-in and eliminated. Today, we have realized that wetlands are a valuable resource that help protect our environment while providing a refuge for wildlife.   Many migratory birds rely on wetlands to rest and regain strength. Certain fish and crab species use wetlands as a place to grow. Continued destruction of wetlands will lead to a string of untold woes both for man and for the variety of animals that depend on this fast disappearing and little-known habitat.

ANIMALS *of the* WETLANDS

Crocodylus mindorensis

PHILIPPINE ◆ CROCODILE

Buwaya

Endemic

Class: Reptilia

Length: 2.5 to 3.5 m

Range: Reported on Mindoro,

Jolo & Busuanga only

This reptile can be found only on Mindoro, Jolo and northern Palawan in the Philippines. Though not as large as the Estuarine Crocodile, it is widely known for its ferocity. This crocodile submerges itself and slows down its heart to six beats a minute while waiting for its prey. Then, in a flash, it streaks to the surface and attacks. This specimen, is from the Silliman Marine Lab on the island of Negros.

TAN

TAN

WHITE ◆ BREASTED
SEA ◆ EAGLE

63

Crocodylus porosus

ESTUARINE ◆ CROCODILE

Buwaya

Class: Reptilia

Length: 4.5 to 6 m

Range: Indo-Pacific Region

and Australia

Manila Zoo, Manila

Crocodiles are the largest of all living reptiles. The largest crocodile ever captured was from Laguna de Bay in the Philippines. It was an Estuarine Crocodile that is estimated to be 21 feet long. That specimen was killed by a Frenchman named Paul de la Gironiere who had the foresight to send its skull to the Agassiz Museum in Harvard. The Estuarine Crocodile can be found in various parts of the Indo-Pacific Region.

TAN

BRAHMINY ◆ KITE

TAN

SAIL ◆ FIN ◆ LIZARD

TAN

TAN

PHILIPPINE ◆ MALLARD

TAN

WHISTLING ◆ GREEN ◆ PIGEON

LITTLE MANGROVE HERON

TAN

RUFOUS ◆ NIGHT ◆ HERON

TAN

• Manila Zoo, Manila

35 Palm Civet • *Paradoxurus hermaphroditus Alamid* • Class: Mammalia • Length: 92 to 97 cm • Range: Throughout the Philippines • Manila Zoo, Manila

32 Phil Horned Owl • *Bubo philippensis Kuago* • Class: Aves • Size: 40 to 50 cm • Range: Endemic – Luzon, Mindanao, Cebu, Leyte • Manila Zoo, Manila

31 Visayan Spotted Deer • *Cervus alfredi Usa* • Class: Mammalia • Height: 139 to 142 cm at shoulder • Status: ENDANGERED • Range: Endemic – Reported on Negros, Leyte & Samar only • Silliman University, Negros Oriental

Animals of the Coral Reefs & Seas

54 Banded Sea Snake • *Hydrophis* • *Ahas Dagat* • Class: Reptilia

53 Barracuda • *Sphyraena barracuda* • *Tursilyo* • Class: Pisces • Apo Reef, Mindoro

47 Blue Spotted Sting Ray • *Pagi* • Tubbataha Reef, Sulu Sea • Class: Pisces

58 Chambered Nautilus • *Nautilus pompilius* • Class: Cephalopoda • Apo Reef, Mindoro

56 Christmas Tree Worm • *Spirobranchus* • Class: Polychaeta

44 Cleaner Shrimp • *Stenopus* • Class: Crustacea

56 Crown of Thorns Starfish • *Acanthaster planci* • Class: Asteroidea

48 Cuttlefish • *Sepia officinalis* • *Pusit lumot* • Class: Cephalopoda • Busuanga, Palawan

45 Dugong • *Dugong dugon* • *Duyong* • Class: Mammalia • Size: 2 to 2.5 m • Status: ENDANGERED • Range: Reported in

Palawan, Bicol and Samar • Haribon Foundation

56 Feather Star • *Comasteridae* • Class: Crinoidea

40 Giant Clam • *Taklobo* • Class: Bivalvia • Size: 1.5 m • Status: THREATENED • Range: Tropic Seas

41 Green Sea Turtle • *Chelonia mydas* • *Pawikan* • Class: Reptilia • Length: 75 to 80 cm • Status: ENDANGERED • Range: Tropic Seas• Calauit Wildlife Sanctuary, Palawan

42 Hawksbill Turtle • *Eretmochelys imbricata Pawikan, Karaan* • Class: Reptilia • Length: 70 to 75 cm • Status: ENDANGERED • Range: Tropic Seas

54 Lionfish • *Pterois volitans* • Class: Pisces

57 Long spined black Sea Urchin • *Diadema setosum* • Class: Echinoidea

46 Manta Ray • *Mobula diabolus* • Class: Pisces Width: 3 to 6 m • Range: Tropic Seas • Tubbataha Reef, Sulu Sea

44 Moray Eel • *Symbranchydae Muraenidae* • *Igat* • Class: Pisces

51 Porcupine Globefish • *Diodon* • *Butete* • Class: Pisces

50 Clown Anemonefish • *Amphiprion ocellaris* • Class: Pisces

57 Sea Urchin • *Echinometra mathaei* • *Suwaki* • Class: Echinoidea

55 Smooth Trunkfish • *Ostracion* • Class: Pisces

43 Whale Shark • *Rhincodon typus* • Class: Selachii • Size: 12 to 15 m • Status: RARE • Range: Tropic Seas

Animals of the Wetlands

65 Brahminy Kite • *Haliastur indus Intermedius Lawin* • Class: Aves • Size: 46 cm Status: COMMON • Range: India to Solomon Islands, throughout the Philippines • Manila Zoo, Manila

64 Estuarine Crocodile • *Crocodylus porosus Buwaya* • Class: Reptilia • Length: 4.5 to 6 m • Status: ENDANGERED • Range: Indo-Pacific Region and Australia • Manila Zoo, Manila

68 Little Mangrove Heron • *Butorides striatus javensis* • *Bakau Itim* • Class: Aves • Size: 40 – 47.5 cm • Range: Throughout the Philippines & all over Asia • Manila Zoo, Manila

62 Philippine Crocodile • *Crocodylus mindorensis* •*Buwaya* • Class: Reptilia • Length: 2.5 to 3.5 m • Status: ENDANGERED • Range: Endemic – Reported on Mindoro, Jolo & Busuanga only • Silliman University, Negros Or.

68 Philippine Mallard • *Anas luzonica* • *Dumara* • Class: Aves • Size: 50 cm • Status: THREATENED • Range: Endemic to the Philippines, widely distributed • Manila Zoo, Manila

69 Rufous Night Heron • *Nycticorax caledonicus manilensis* • *Bakau Gabi* • Class: Aves • Size: 62 cm • Range: Throughout the Philippines & on many Pacific Islands • Manila Zoo, Manila

69 Sail-finned Lizard • *Iguana* • *Hydrosaurus pustulosus* • Class: Reptilia • Length: 60 cm • Status: THREATENED • Manila Zoo, Manila

68 Whistling Green Pigeon • *Treron formosae* • *Vuyit* • Class: Aves • Range: Batanes, Babuyan Islands & Taiwan • Itbud, Batanes

63 White Breasted Sea Eagle • *Haliaectus leucogaster* • *Agila* • Class: Aves • Size: 75 cm • Status: THREATENED • Range: Throughout the

Philippines, Indochina, Malay Peninsula, & Australia • Manila Zoo, Manila

BIBLIOGRAPHY

Alcala, A. C. *Philippine Land Vertebrates*, New Day Publishers, Q.C., 1976.

Attenborough, D., *Life On Earth, A Natural History*, Little, Brown & Co., Boston, 1979.

Farino, T., *The Living World*, Mallard Press, New York, 1989.

Gironiere, P.P. de la, *Twenty Years in the Philippines*, Harper & Brothers, New York, 1854.

Gonzales, P. & Rees, C., *Birds of the Philippines*, Haribon Foundation, Philippines, 1988.

Graham, A. & Beard, P., *Eyelids of Morning, The Mingled Destinies of Crocodiles & Men*, Chronicle Books, San Francisco, 1990.

Heck, J.G., *The Complete Encyclopedia of Illustration*, Crown Publisher, USA, 1979

Oliver, A.P.H., *The Hamlyn Guide to Shells of the World*, Hamlyn Publishing Group, U.K., 1981.

Rabor, D.S., *Philippine Reptiles and Amphibians*, Abiva Publishing House, Inc., Manila, 1981.

Springsteen, F.J. & Leobrera, F.M., *Shells of the Philipines*, Carfel Seashell Museum, Manila, 1986.

Ulrich-Bernard, Hans, *Southeast Asia Wildlife*, APA Publications (HK) Ltd., 1991.

White, A.T., *Philippine Coral Reefs, A Natural History Guide*, New Day Publishers, Quezon City, 1987.

A C K N O W L E D G E M E N T S

ASIAN WETLAND BUREAU, CEBU
Perla Magsalay

◆

CRMF/CALAUIT WILDLIFE SANCTUARY, PALAWAN
Conrad Micaller, Jr., Dr. Frank Panol, Johnny Gapus,
Froilan Sariego, Rose Labis, the Calauit Staff

◆

DEPARTMENT OF TOURISM
Sec. Narzalina Lim, Betty Nelle, Bong Bengzon

◆

ERDB-DENR WILDLIFE BREEDING CENTER, MT. MAKILING
Dir. Carlos C. Tomboc, Ruben Callo, Sim Pasicolan
the ERDB Staff at Los Bañ os

◆

HARIBON FOUNDATION
Cristi Nozawa, Maribeth Reyes-Baril, Oca Lapida

◆

MANILA ZOO
Dr. Silvestre Boton, Dr. Tony Bascug, Dr. Bob Deblois,
the Manila Zoo Staff

◆

NATIONAL MUSEUM
Dr. Jess Peralta, Pete Gonzales

◆

PHILIPPINE EAGLE RESEACH & NATURE CENTER, DAVAO
Stephen Paspe, Lito Serenio, Doming Tadena

◆

SILLIMAN UNIVERSITY, DUMAGUETE
Dr. Angel Alcala, Dr. Ely Alcala, Louella Dolar

◆

FRIENDS
Gaji Abela, Robert Alejandro, Juny Binamira, Carina Escudero, Kukay Fragante,
Claudia Itchon & her group of Calauit volunteers,
Mike & Yasuko Jones, Beth Parrocha, Gerry Reyes, Elizabeth Reyes, Didith Tan,
Iggy Tan, George Tapan, Gilbert & Gerard Uy-Matiao